Bath Bombs

A Step-by-Step Beginner's Guide to Making Simple, Homemade Bath Bombs + 50 Luxurious DIY Bath Bombs

Dianne Selton

© 2016

Dianne Selton Copyright © 2016

All rights reserved. No part of this publication may be reproduced, distributed, or transmitted in any form or by any means, including photocopying, recording, or other electronic or mechanical methods, without the prior written permission of the publisher, except in the case of brief quotations embodied in critical reviews and certain other noncommercial uses permitted by copyright law.

Although the author and publisher have made every effort to ensure that the information in this book was correct at press time, the author and publisher do not assume and hereby disclaim any liability to any party for any loss, damage, or disruption caused by errors or omissions, whether such errors or omissions result from negligence, accident, or any other cause.

Table of Contents

Introduction

Bath-Bombs 1-20

Bath Bombs 21-40

Bath Bomb 40-49

Bath Bomb 50

Storing and Gifting Your Bath Bombs

Conclusion

Introduction

Bath bombs have amazing healing abilities, and yet they're luxurious and great gifts for the holiday season. If you want a bath bomb to 'explode' you'll want to put them directly under the faucet when you start to draw your bath. They'll start to fizz, and it makes it seem like a day spa adventure. A good bath bomb is meant to be fragrant, and it's meant to relax all of your muscles.

Bath bombs are therapeutic, and you don't always have to buy them from the store. In this book, you'll learn how to make simple and easy bath bombs. When you're searching online, you may find that some bath bombs are better than others. This book has done all of the work for you. It's already been sorted what is and isn't a good recipe, and only the good has been included. It allows you to relax and become reinvigorated so that you can face another day.

Slhopping List:

Once you're ready to go on your own bath bomb making adventure, you'll need to have some equipment on hand. It'll help to make sure that everything goes smoothly and you don't have to stop what you're doing to continue. Remember that bath bombs make great gifts or personal luxury.

- Cornstarch: This is what will help to control the fizzing reaction while you mix your bath bombs.

- Baking Soda: You'll want food grade, and do not get technical grade. Technical grade has unwanted impurities, and it is much coarser looking.

- Essential Oils: You can find these at any health food store or even craft stores. If you can't find the one you're looking for, then you can always go online. These will be what causes the fragrance in your bath bombs.

- Citric Acid: If you go to a wine making supplier, then you'll be able to find citric acid. Of course, you can also find them at some spice shops, online, or even some supermarkets if you're willing to look. You will want super-fine granules (about the size of table salt), and do not use the powder. The powder is too volatile.

- Witch Hazel: This is often used in the spritzer bottle. Water can set off the bath bomb, but when you use witch hazel it'll moisten it enough without doing so. Water can work in its place, but you may make mistakes.

- Rubber Gloves: You'll want to have rubber gloves due to the citric acid being a skin irritant. This will help to make sure that you do not have any issues.

- Accessories: Spritzer bottle, glass or plastic mixing bowl, and molds of your choice are also needed.

Molds:

You'll see that soap molds work just fine for bath bombs, and you'll want to pack your bath bombs in your molds. However, make sure that you don't pack them too tightly. Otherwise, when you get them out, your bath bombs will crack. It's a balancing act. You want to pack them tight enough that you get the design, but too tight and you'll have a few break on you. These may not be great for gifts, but they can still be used.

Some Bath Bomb Benefits

You may be wondering what bath bombs can really do for you, but there's no reason to wonder. Bath bombs have well known benefits that will help you to relax, stave off anxiety, and so much more. You'll find various bath bombs benefits listed below.

- **They're Relaxing:** This is the main benefit of bath bombs. They're meant to help transform your bathing experience into something that's right out of a spa. Everyone has built up stress, and this can lead to much worse ailments. It's important to relieve stress. Nothing is better than being able to just relax in your tub without a care in the world. This can be hard, but with the right mixture, bath bombs can help you to forget everything.

- **It's a Detox:** Bath bombs have benefits for your skin as well. Baking soda will actually help to detox your skin, which will help with your overall complexion. You'll find that the Epsom salts used in these bath bombs will have that affect as well. Even the Dead Sea salt will help to exfoliate and detox your skin.

- **Relieve Muscle Tension:** Bath bombs are known to help to relieve muscle tension and soreness. This makes them useful after a workout or just a stressful day. Some bath bombs will help with this more than others, of course.

- **Therapeutic:** Bath bombs, when made with essential oils, can be therapeutic. They can help you to get through tough times by relieving depression and anxiety. It even gives you time to think, and some essential oils are known to help to clear your head. Essential oils are commonly used as a form of aromatherapy.

Bath Bombs 1-20

Bath Bomb #1 Mandarin Sweet Orange

Ingredients:

1. 1 Cup Baking Soda
2. ¾ Cup Corn Starch
3. ½ Cup Citric Acid, Powdered
4. 2 Teaspoons Mandarin Essential Oil
5. Yellow Food Coloring
6. Red Food Coloring

Directions:

1. Take the cornstarch, powdered citric acid, and baking soda, combining them in a bowl. Make sure it's completely mixed.

2. Take your mandarin essential oil, adding it in slowly. You'll need to pause to stir frequently. Add in a few drops of yellow and red food coloring. You'll need to have two drops of yellow to every drop of red. This will make it a bright orange.

3. Take the mixture, pressing it firmly into whatever mold you've chosen. Take your witch hazel to moisten it if it gets too dry.

4. Let dry overnight, and then remove from the molds gently before storing.

Bath Bomb #2 Fresh Lemon

Ingredients:

1. 1 Cup Baking Soda
2. ¾ Cup Cornstarch
3. ½ Cup Citric Acid, Powdered
4. 1 Teaspoon Spearmint Essential Oil
5. 1 ½ Teaspoon Lemon Eucalyptus Essential Oil

Directions:

1. Take all of your dry ingredients, combining them together in your mixing bowl so that there are no clumps.
2. Pour your essential oils carefully into the mixture, stirring.
3. Add in a few spritz of witch hazel to keep the ingredients moist, but stir to make sure it doesn't interact.
4. Place in molds of your choice, and then let dry completely overnight. Store carefully.

Bath Bomb #3 Tea Tree Bomb

Ingredients:

1. ¼ Cup baking Soda
2. ¼ Cup Citric Acid, Powdered
3. ½ Cup Cornstarch
4. 3 Tablespoon Almond Oil
5. 3 Tablespoons Coconut Oil
6. ¼ Cup Shea Butter
7. 2 Teaspoons Tea Tree Essential Oil

Directions:

1. Take all of your dry ingredients and place them in a mixing bowl. Stir carefully. You'll need to fold in your coconut oil and shea butter to get the proper consistency.
2. Add in your almond oil next, and stir frequently to avoid fizzing.
3. You'll then take your molds, pressing it into it gently. Spritz as necessary with witch hazel. Let dry overnight, and then store properly.

Bath Bomb #4 Vanilla & Orange

Ingredients:

1. 1 Cup Baking Soda
2. ¾ Cup Cornstarch
3. ½ Cup Citric Acid, Powdered
4. 1 Teaspoon Vanilla Essential Oil
5. 1 Teaspoon Sweet Orange Essential Oil

Directions:

1. Place all dry ingredients into a bowl, mixing thoroughly. It should have a uniform consistency.
2. Pour in your essential oils slowly while stirring. Add food coloring if desired, and then stir more.
3. Pack into molds, spritzing if necessary.
4. Let dry overnight before storing.

Bath Bomb #5 Lemon Twist

Ingredients:

1. ¾ Cup Cornstarch
2. 1 Teaspoon Almond Oil
3. ½ Cup Citric Acid, Powdered
4. 1 Cup Baking Soda
5. 1 Teaspoon Lemon Essential Oil

6. 1 Teaspoon Lime Essential Oil
7. Yellow Food Coloring
8. Green Food Coloring

Directions:

1. Take all of your dry ingredients, mixing in your mixing bowl. Make sure it's stirred well.
2. Add in your almond oil, stirring, and then pour in your essential oils slowly. Make sure to stir until combined.
3. Separate your mixture into two different bowls. Add green food coloring in one and yellow in the next.
4. Place into molds, keeping your yellow and green separate. Let dry overnight before stirring. Spritz as necessary to keep it from drying out.

Bath Bomb #6 Soothing White Tea

Ingredients:

1. 1 Cup Baking Soda
2. ½ Cup Cornstarch
3. ½ Cup Citric Acid
4. 2 Tablespoons Epsom Salt

5. 2 Tablespoons Coconut Oil
6. 2 Tablespoons Strong White Tea
7. 1 Teaspoon Lavender Essential Oil

Directions:

1. Brew your white tea strongly, and then wait for it to cool completely.
2. You'll then take all of your dry ingredients, mixing them into a bowl before there aren't any clumps.
3. Add in your coconut oil slowly, whisking it until it's worked through completely.
4. Add in your white tea slowly, and then add in your essential oil slowly. It should be one spoonful at a time.
5. Press into molds, spritzing as necessary, and then wait for it to dry overnight before packing.

Bath Bomb #7 Luxurious Skin

Ingredients:

1. ½ Cup Cornstarch
2. ¼ Cup Baking Soda
3. ¼ Cup Citric Acid, Powdered

4. ¼ Cup Shea Butter
5. 3 Tablespoons Coconut Oil
6. 3 Tablespoons Almond Oil
7. 2 Teaspoons Carrot Seed Essential Oil

Directions:

1. Add all dry ingredients into your mixing bowl, and mix thoroughly.
2. Work the shea butter and coconut oil in carefully.
3. Add in your almond oil and carrot seed oil one teaspoon at a time. Mix slowly and thoroughly.
4. Press into molds, spritzing as necessary. Let it dry overnight and then store.

Bath Bomb #8 Relaxing Lavender

Ingredients:

1. 1 Cup Baking Soda
2. 1 Cup Citric Acid, Powdered
3. ¼ Cup Epsom Salt
4. ½ Cup Cornstarch
5. ¼ Cup Epsom Salt

6. ¼ Cup Powdered Milk
7. 2 Tablespoons Cocoa Butter, Softened
8. 2 Tablespoons Almond Oil
9. 2 Teaspoons Lavender Essential Oil
10. Blue Food Coloring
11. Red Food Coloring

Directions:

1. Take all of your dry ingredients, placing them in your glass or plastic mixing bowl. Make sure you stir well.
2. Add in your cocoa butter, folding it in so that it becomes part of the mixture.
3. Take your almond oil and lavender essential oil, pouring it in slowly. Stir frequently, pausing as necessary.
4. Pour in one drop blue to one drop red food coloring as necessary to create a proper purple tone. Spray with your spritzer if it starts to dry out.
5. Place into molds overnight to let dry before storing.

Bath Bomb #9 Milk & Honey

Ingredients:

1. 1 Cup Baking Soda
2. 1 Cup Citric Acid, Powdered
3. ½ Cup Cornstarch
4. 2 Tablespoons Cocoa Butter, Softened
5. ½ Cup Powdered Milk
6. 2 Tablespoons Olive Oil
7. 1 Teaspoon Beeswax Essential Oil

Directions:

1. Place all of your dry ingredients together in your mixing bowl, mixing until uniform.
2. Pour in your olive oil and cocoa butter, stirring as needed.
3. Add in your beeswax essential oil a little bit at a time, spritzing as necessary to make the mixture workable again.
4. Place firmly into molds overnight to dry before storing.

Bath Bomb #10 The Wake Up Call

Ingredients:

1. 1 Cup Baking Soda
2. ½ Cup Cornstarch

3. 1 Cup Citric Acid, Powdered
4. ¼ Cup Powdered Milk
5. ¼ Cup Epsom Salt
6. 2 Tablespoons Cocoa Butter, Softened
7. 2 Teaspoons Coffee Essential Oil
8. 2 Tablespoons Almond Oil

Directions:

1. Take all of your dry ingredients, mixing together completely.
2. Add in your cocoa butter, folding it in until completely mixed.
3. Take your almond and coffee oil, mixing in gently.
4. Spritz the mixture to keep it from drying out, and then press into molds. Let dry before storing.

Bath Bomb #11 Flowers & Honey

Ingredients:

1. ¾ Cup Cornstarch
2. 1 Cup Baking Soda
3. ½ Cup Citric Acid, Powdered

4. 1 Teaspoon Neroli Essential Oil
5. 1 Teaspoon Beeswax Essential Oil
6. Yellow Food Coloring
7. Honeycomb Mold

Directions:

1. Mix all dry ingredients together, whisking until fully mixed in your bowl.
2. Add your essential oils in a little at a time, slowly.
3. Add in your food coloring, and then spritz as necessary to keep moist.
4. Put in molds to let dry before storing.

Bath Bomb #12 Just Jasmine

Ingredients:

1. 1 Cup Baking Soda
2. ½ Cup Citric Acid, Powdered
3. ¾ Cup Cornstarch
4. 2 Teaspoons Jasmine Essential Oil
5. Jasmine Flowers, Dried

Directions:

1. Mix all dry ingredients together, stirring thoroughly in your mixing bowl.
2. Add in your jasmine essential oil slowly, and make sure it's stirred completely.
3. Place dried flowers in the bottom of your molds.
4. Spritz your mixture to keep it from drying out and then place in the molds.
5. Let dry before storing.

Bath Bomb #13 Relaxing Rejuvenation

Ingredients:

1. ½ Cup Citric Acid, Powdered
2. 1 Cup Baking Soda
3. ¾ Cup Cornstarch
4. 1 Teaspoon Cypress Essential Oil
5. 1 Teaspoon Yuzu Essential Oil

Directions:

1. Take all dry ingredients, mixing together before slowly pouring in your essential oils.
2. Add moisture by spritzing as necessary.
3. Press into mold and let dry before storing.

Bath Bomb #14 Fresh Lemongrass

Ingredients:

1. 1 Cup Baking Soda
2. ½ Cup Citric Acid, Powdered
3. ¾ Cup Cornstarch
4. 1 Teaspoon Lemongrass Essential Oil
5. 1 Teaspoon Cardamom Essential Oil
6. Green Food Coloring

Directions:

1. Mix all of your dry ingredients in a bowl until combined.
2. Add in your essential oils one teaspoon at a time. Pause to mix to avoid clumping, spritzing as needed to keep the mixture pliable.
3. Add in food coloring until you get a light, vibrant green throughout.
4. Press into molds, letting dry before storing.

Bath Bomb #15 Balanced & Bold

Ingredients:

1. ¾ Cup Cornstarch
2. ½ Cup Citric Acid, Powdered
3. 1 Cup Baking Soda
4. 2 Tablespoons Almond Oil
5. 1 Teaspoons Vetiver Essential Oil
6. Red Food Coloring

Directions:

1. Take all of your dry ingredients, mixing them together.
2. Pour your oils in carefully and slowly, stirring frequently.
3. Add in green food coloring or food coloring of choice until you get the shade you like.
4. Spritz as needed to keep pliable, and then put it in your mold. Let dry completely before storing.

Bath Bomb #16 Peace & Love

Ingredients:

1. 1 Cup Baking Soda
2. ½ Cup Citric Acid, Powdered
3. ¼ Cup Dead Sea Salt

4. ½ Cup Cornstarch
5. 3 Tablespoons Coconut Oil
6. 2 Tablespoons Almond Oil
7. 1 Teaspoon Patchouli Essential Oil
8. 1 Teaspoon Oakmoss Essential Oil

Directions:

1. Mix all dry ingredients together in your bowl before adding in your coconut oil. Make sure it's folded in and mixed thoroughly.
2. Add in your almond oil and essential oil, stirring frequently.
3. Spritz your mixture to keep it from drying out, and then place in molds to dry before storing.

Bath Bomb #17 Becoming Basil

Ingredients:

1. 1 Cup Baking Soda
2. ½ Cup Citric Acid, Powdered
3. ½ Cup Cornstarch
4. 2 ¾ Tablespoons Almond Oil
5. ¾ Tablespoons Water

6. 1 Teaspoon Basil Essential Oil

7. 1 Teaspoon Cyprus Essential Oil

Directions:

1. Place all dry ingredients together in your mixing bowl. Mix thoroughly and then set it aside.

2. Mix all of your liquids together in a spate bowl.

3. Add your liquid mixture to your dry mixture slowly to avoid fizzing. Pause to blend often. Spritz if needed.

4. Place into molds to dry before storing.

Bath Bomb #18 Wake Me Up Ginger

Ingredients:

1. ½ Cup Cornstarch

2. ¼ Cup Baking Soda

3. ¼ Cup Citric Acid, Powdered

4. 6 Tablespoons Shea Butter

5. 3 Tablespoons Almond Oil

6. 3 Tablespoons Coconut Oil

7. 1 Teaspoon Ginger Essential Oil

8. Red Food Coloring
9. Yellow food Coloring

Directions:

1. Mix all of your dry ingredients in your mixing bowl thoroughly.
2. Add in your coconut oil and shea butter a little at a time. Don't stop until you've achieved a uniform consistency.
3. Then add in your ginger essential oil and almond oil slowly. Add a few drops of food coloring.
4. Spritz if it gets too dry, and then place into molds to dry before storing.

Bath Bomb #19 Incense Delight

Ingredients:

1. 1 Cup Baking soda
2. ¾ Cup Cornstarch
3. ½ Cup Citric Acid, Powdered
4. ¼ Cup Epsom Salt
5. 3 Tablespoon Coconut Oil
6. 2 Tablespoons Almond Oil
7. 1 Teaspoon Bay Essential Oil

8. 1 Teaspoon Sandalwood Essential Oil

Directions:

1. Combine all of your dry ingredients in your bowl before working in your coconut oil. Make sure it's mixed thoroughly.
2. Add in your oils, and add in food coloring if necessary. A brown color is recommended.
3. Spritz to make sure it is the consistency of wet sand, and then place into molds. Let dry before storing.

Bath Bomb #20 Red Currants

Ingredients:

1. 1 Cup Baking Soda
2. ½ Cup Citric Acid, Powdered
3. ¼ Cup Cornstarch
4. ½ Cup Epsom Salts
5. 1 Teaspoon Lavender Essential Oil
6. 2 ¾ Tablespoons Almond Oil
7. ¾ Tablespoons Water
8. 1 Teaspoon Red Currant Essential Oil

Directions:

1. Combine all of your dry ingredients, and then take all of your liquid ingredients to mix together in a separate bowl.

2. Combine both mixtures together slowly to avoid fizzing.

3. Press firmly into your molds, and then let dry. Store only once dry.

Bath Bombs #21-40

Bath Bomb #21 Energizing Rosemary

Ingredients:

1. ¾ Cup Cornstarch
2. ¾ Cup Epsom Salts
3. 1 ¼ Cup Baking Soda
4. ¾ Cup Citric Acid, Powdered
5. 4 Teaspoons Coconut Oil
6. 4 Teaspoons Water
7. 6 Teaspoons Rosemary Essential Oil
8. 6 Teaspoons Mint Essential Oil
9. Dried Rosemary

Directions:

1. Take all of your dry ingredients, mixing together in a bowl.
2. Add in your coconut oil, folding until you reach a uniform consistency.
3. Add in water, rosemary essential oil, and mint essential oil carefully. Spritz only if necessary.

4. Place rosemary at the bottom of your molds, and then place your mixture into your molds. Pack tightly, and store only when completely dry.

Bath Bomb #22 Peppy Peppermint

Ingredients:

1. 1 Cup Baking Soda
2. ½ Cup Citric Acid, Powdered
3. ½ Cup Cornstarch
4. ½ Cup Epsom Salts
5. 2 Teaspoons Peppermint Essential Oil
6. 2 ½ Teaspoons Almond Oil
7. Red Food Coloring

Directions:

1. Take all dry ingredients, mixing them together.
2. Take your peppermint essential oil and almond oil. Mix together, spritzing as necessary to get the consistency of wet sand.
3. Add in food coloring, and then place into molds. Let dry before storing.

Bath Bomb #23 Simply Vanilla

Ingredients:

1. 2 Teaspoons Vanilla Essential Oil
2. ½ Cup Citric Acid, Powdered
3. 1 ¼ Cup Baking Soda
4. 2 Teaspoons Almond Oil

Directions:

1. Take all of your dry ingredients, mixing together.
2. Add in your almond oil and vanilla essential oil slowly.
3. Spritz as necessary, placing into molds.
4. Let dry overnight before storing.

Bath Bomb #24 Relaxing Night

Ingredients:

1. 2 Tablespoons Shea Butter, Melted
2. 1 Cup Baking Soda
3. ½ Cup Citric Acid, Powdered
4. ½ Cup Tapioca Powder
5. 1/3 Cup Epsom Salt

6. 1 Teaspoon Eucalyptus Essential Oil
7. 1 Teaspoon Witch Hazel, Dried
8. ½ Teaspoon Chamomile Essential Oil
9. ½ Teaspoon Lavender Essential Oil

Directions:

1. Take all of your dry ingredients, including your dried witch hazel, and mix them together in a bowl.
2. Add in your melted shea butter, making sure it's completely mixed. Fold until you've made a uniform mixture.
3. Add in your essential oils, mixing thoroughly.
4. Spritz if necessary, and then press into molds. Let dry before storing.

Bath Bomb #25 Happy Tangerine

Ingredients:

1. ½ Cup Cornstarch
2. ½ Cup Citric Acid, Powdered
3. 1 Cup Baking Soda
4. ½ Cup Epsom Salts
5. 3 Tablespoon Almond Oil

6. 1 Teaspoon Grapefruit Essential Oil
7. 1 Teaspoon Tangerine Essential Oil

Directions:

1. Mix all of your dry ingredients together.
2. Add in your liquids ingredient slowly, pausing to stir as necessarily. You must do this slowly to avoid fizzing.
3. Spritz if needed to keep at a wet sand consistency before placing into molds.
4. Let dry before storing.

Bath Bomb #26 Cheery Citrus

Ingredients:

1. 1 Cup Baking Soda
2. ½ Cup Citric Acid, Powdered
3. 1 Tablespoon Shea Butter, Melted
4. 1 Teaspoon Grapefruit Essential Oil
5. Blue Food Coloring

Ingredients:

1. Mix your baking soda and citric acid together, and then add in your shea butter slowly, mixing until combined thoroughly.

2. Add in your grapefruit citrus oil slowly to avoid fizzing.

3. Add in your blue food coloring, spritzing with your witch hazel solution as needed to keep moist.

4. Place into molds and let dry. Store once fully dry.

Bath Bomb #27 Healing Apple

Ingredients:

1. 1 Cup Baking Soda
2. ½ Cup Cornstarch
3. ½ Cup Citric Acid
4. ½ Cup Epsom Salts
5. 2 ¾ Tablespoon Almond Oil
6. 1 Teaspoon Raspberry Essential Oil
7. 1 Teaspoon Apple Essential Oil

Directions:

1. Combine all of your dry ingredients together.
2. Add in your essential oils and almond oils slowly. It should be one teaspoon at a time to avoid premature fizzing.

3. Spritz if needed to make the consistency of damp sand.
4. Place into molds, letting dry overnight before storing.

Bath Bomb #28 The Restful Rose

Ingredients:

1. 1 Cup Baking Soda
2. ½ Cup Citric Acid, Powdered
3. 1 Cup Cornstarch
4. 2 Tablespoons Almond Oil
5. 2 Tablespoons Coconut Oil
6. 3 Ounces Cocoa Butter, Softened
7. 4 Teaspoons Rose Essential Oil
8. Rose Petals, Dried

Directions:

1. Take all dry ingredients, mixing them together.
2. Fold in your coconut oil and cocoa butter until completely mixed.
3. Add all essential oils and almond oils slowly.

4. Lay rose petals in the bottom of your molds, and then take your mixture, spritzing if necessary, and place in your molds.
5. Let dry before storing.

Bath Bomb #29 Some Bitter Spice

Ingredients:

1. 1 Cup Baking Soda
2. ¾ Cup Cornstarch
3. ½ Cup Citric Acid, Powdered
4. 1 Teaspoon Black Pepper Essential Oil
5. 1 Teaspoon Bitter Orange Essential Oil
6. Red Food Coloring
7. Yellow Food Coloring
8. Dried Sage
9. Dried Rosemary

Directions:

1. Take all of your dry ingredients except for your herbs, mixing them all together.
2. Mix in your essential oils slowly until fully combined.

3. Add in your food coloring. Two drops yellow to every one drop red.

4. Spritz if necessary to keep at a wet sand consistency. Put your dried herbs in the bottom of your molds.

5. Place your mixture into your molds, and only store once completely dry.

Bath Bomb #30 Excited Cinnamon

Ingredients:

1. 2 Tablespoons Baking Soda
2. 1 Tablespoon Citric Acid, Powdered
3. 1 Tablespoon Cornstarch
4. ¾ Teaspoon Cinnamon Tea, Brewed Strong
5. 1 Tablespoon Epsom Salts
6. Red Food Coloring
7. ¼ Teaspoon Olive Oil

Directions:

1. Start by brewing a strong cup of cinnamon tea. You'll need to let it cool down completely before using.
2. Whisk together all of your dry ingredients.

3. Slowly add in your tea, adding one to two drops of your red food coloring as well. Continue to mix to create a wet sand consistency.

4. Spritz if needed and press into your molds. Let dry completely before storing.

Bath Bomb #31 Passion Flower

Ingredients:

1. 1 Cup Baking Soda
2. ½ Cup Cornstarch
3. ½ Cup Citric Acid, Powdered
4. ½ Cup Epsom Salts
5. 2 ¾ Tablespoons Almond Oil
6. 1 Teaspoon Passionflower Essential Oil
7. 1 Teaspoon Ylang-Ylang Essential Oil

Directions:

1. Mix all dry ingredients together, and then add in your essential oils and almond oils one teaspoon at a time. Mix thoroughly until combined.

2. Spritz if necessary to keep the consistency of wet sand before placing into molds.

3. Make sure that you let dry completely before storing.

Bath Bomb #32 Green Tea Delight

Ingredients:

1. 2 Tablespoons Baking Soda
2. 1 Tablespoon Citric Acid, Powdered
3. 1 Tablespoon Epsom Salts
4. 1 Tablespoon Cornstarch
5. ¼ Teaspoon Olive Oil
6. ¾ Teaspoons Green Tea, Brewed Strong
7. Green Food Coloring

Directions:

1. You want to start by brewing your green tea as strong as you can, and then allow for it to completely cool.
2. During the meantime, you can whisk together all of your dry ingredients.
3. Add in your green tea, and then add your olive oil. Mix thoroughly, but be sure not to add it all at once to avoid fizzing.
4. Add in your food coloring to get a nice, light green color. Spritz if needed.

5. Place into molds, and allow to dry completely before storing.

Bath Bomb #33 Autumn Bomb

Ingredients:

1. 1 Cup Baking Soda
2. ¼ Cup Epsom Salt
3. ¾ Cup Cornstarch
4. ½ Cup Citric Acid, Powdered
5. 2 Tablespoons Coconut Oil
6. 1 Teaspoon Cinnamon Essential Oil
7. 1 Teaspoon Ginger Essential Oil
8. ½ Teaspoon Clove Essential Oil
9. ½ Teaspoon Nutmeg Essential Oil
10. Red Food Coloring
11. Yellow Food Coloring
12. Pumpkin Shaped Soap Molds

Directions:

1. Take all of your dry ingredients, mixing them thoroughly before continuing.

2. Work in your coconut oil next, and you'll want to make sure it's mixed completely into your mixture.

3. Take your essential oils, pouring them in slowly. Make sure to stir each and every spoonful as you only pour one spoonful at a time.

4. Add three drops of yellow food coloring to each two drops of the red that you mix. This will make a nice orange. Keep doing so until you reach the desired shade of orange.

5. Spritz if needed, and then place into your pumpkin shaped molds to dry. Let dry completely before storing.

Bath Bomb #34 Winter Bomb

Ingredients:

1. ¼ Cup Citric Acid, Powdered
2. ½ Cup Baking Soda
3. ¼ Cup Cornstarch
4. ¼ Cup Epsom Salt
5. 2 ½ Teaspoons Almond Oil
6. 1 Teaspoon Spearmint Essential Oil
7. 1 Teaspoon Fir Needle Essential Oil

8. Blue Food Coloring

Directions:

1. Mix together all of your dry ingredients, making sure to mix thoroughly to avoid clumps.

2. Slowly add in your wet ingredients, stirring until completely mixed together. Spritz if needed to get the right consistency.

3. Add in your food coloring until you get a light shade of blue. One to two drops will usually work.

4. Press into molds and let dry overnight before storing.

Bath Bomb #35 Seasonal Spice

Ingredients:

1. 1 Cup Baking Soda
2. 2/3 Cup Citric Acid, Powdered
3. ½ Cup Epsom Salt
4. 2 Teaspoons Beetroot Powder
5. 1 Tablespoon Almond Oil
6. 1 Teaspoon Orange Essential Oil
7. ¾ Teaspoon Cinnamon Essential Oil

8. 1 ¼ Teaspoon Fir Needle Essential Oil

Directions:

1. Place all of your dry ingredients into a bowl and mix together until the mixture is uniform.
2. Add in your almond oil, stirring completely before adding one teaspoon of essential oil at a time, mixing after each.
3. Add more beetroot powder if you want a brighter red, and spritz if necessary to keep the consistency of wet sand.
4. Place into molds to dry overnight before storing.

Bath Bomb #36 Ginger & Peach

Ingredients:

1. 1 Cup Baking Soda
2. ½ Cup Citric Acid, Powdered
3. ½ Cup Cornstarch
4. ½ Cup Dead Sea Salt
5. 1 Teaspoon Peach Essential Oil
6. 1 Teaspoon Ginger Essential Oil
7. 2 ½ Tablespoons Almond Oil

Directions:

1. Mix all of your dry ingredients together thoroughly before continuing.
2. Add in your liquid ingredients slowly, making sure to stir and mix slowly to avoid fizzing.
3. Spritz with your solution if needed, placing your mixture into molds.
4. Let sit overnight before storing. It should dry completely.

Bath Bomb #37 Blackberry Blast

Ingredients:

1. 1 Cup Baking Soda
2. ½ Cup Citric Acid, Powdered
3. ½ Cup Cornstarch
4. ½ Cup Epsom Salts
5. 1 ½ Teaspoon Blackberry Essential Oil
6. ½ Teaspoon Vanilla Essential Oil
7. 2 ½ Tablespoons Almond Oil

Directions:

1. Mix all of your dry ingredients together, and then place your liquid ingredients in slowly. Make sure to pause and mix to avoid fizzing.
2. Place into molds, allowing to dry completely before storing.

Bath Bomb #38 Simple Luxury

Ingredients:

1. 1 Tablespoon Cornstarch
2. 2 Tablespoons Baking Soda
3. ½ Tablespoon Citric Acid, Powdered
4. ¼ Teaspoon Avocado Oil
5. 1 Tablespoon Epsom Salt
6. ½ Teaspoon Coconut Oil
7. ¼ Teaspoon Frankincense Essential Oil

Directions:

1. Start by combining all of your dry ingredients in a large mixing bowl.
2. Slowly add your liquid ingredients a little at a time. Stir in between to avoid premature fizzing.
3. Spritz if needed, and place into molds to dry before storing.

Bath Bomb #39 Drifting Sleep

Ingredients:

1. 1 Tablespoon Epsom Salt
2. 1 Tablespoon Cornstarch
3. 2 Tablespoons Baking Soda
4. ½ Teaspoon Citric Acid
5. ½ Teaspoon Chamomile Essential Oil
6. ½ Teaspoon Evening Primrose Essential Oil

Directions:

1. Make sure to mix all dry ingredients in your mixing bowl first.
2. Add one essential oil at a time, mixing in between to avoid fizzing.
3. Spritz if needed, placing into molds to dry overnight before storing.

Bath Bomb #40 Flower Explosion

Ingredients:

1. 1 Tablespoon Epsom Salt
2. 2 Tablespoons Baking Soda

3. ½ Tablespoon Citric Acid
4. 1 Tablespoon Cornstarch
5. Pink Food Coloring
6. ¾ Teaspoon Sunflower Oil
7. ¼ Teaspoon Rosehip Essential Oil

Directions:

1. Mix all dry ingredients together first before adding each of your oils in slowly. Make sure to mix slowly before adding more.
2. Add in your pink food coloring. One or two drops will do just fine to produce a light pink color.
3. Spritz if needed before putting into your molds, allowing too dry before storage.

Bath Bomb #40-50

Bath Bomb #41 Mighty Mango

Ingredients:

1. 1 Cup Citric Acid
2. 2 Cup Baking Soda
3. 3 Tablespoons Kaolin Clay
4. 1 Tablespoon Mango Essential Oil
5. 1 Tablespoon Witch Hazel
6. Yellow Food Coloring
7. 4 Tablespoons Shea Butter, Melted

Directions:

1. Combine your dry ingredients in your mixing bowl, making sure it's combined properly.
2. Add your liquid ingredients slowly, stirring in between. You should come out with the consistency of wet sand.
3. Add in your yellow food coloring until you reach the desired shade.
4. Place into molds to dry overnight, spritzing if necessary first.

Bath Bomb #42 Regaining Youth

Ingredients:

1. 1 Cup Citric Acid
2. 2 Cup Baking Soda
3. ¼ Cup Cornstarch
4. ¼ Cup Dead Sea Salt
5. 1 Tablespoon Almond Oil
6. ½ Teaspoon Myrrh Essential Oil
7. ¼ Teaspoon Frankincense Essential Oil
8. 1 Teaspoon Lavender Essential Oil

Directions:

1. Add in your dry ingredients, mixing thoroughly.
2. Add in your liquid ingredients one at a time, making sure to stir in between each to avoid fizzing. Spritz if necessary.
3. Place into molds to dry completely overnight before storing properly.

Bath Bomb #43 Trip to the Sea

Ingredients:

1. 1 Teaspoon Sea Salt

2. 2 Cups Baking Soda
3. 1 Cup Citric Acid
4. ¼ Cup Epsom Salt
5. ¼ Cup Cornstarch
6. 1 Tablespoon Almond Oil
7. 1 Teaspoon Ocean Breeze Fragrance Oil

Directions:

1. Place all of your dry ingredients into the mixing bowl, making sure to thoroughly combine them.
2. Add in your almond oil and ocean breeze fragrance oil slowly, mixing until it's fully combined.
3. Spritz if needed, and place into your molds. Make sure it's completely dry before storing.

Bath Bomb #44 Cream & Cranberries

Ingredients:

1. 1 Cup Citric Acid
2. 2 Cups Baking Soda
3. 4 Tablespoons Almond Oil
4. 1 Tablespoon Witch Hazel

5. 3 Tablespoons Kaolin Clay
6. 1 Tablespoon Cranberry Essential Oil
7. Red Food Coloring

Directions:

1. Take all dry ingredients, placing them in your mixing bowl. Make sure to combine completely.
2. Add in your liquid ingredients slowly. Make sure that you stir in between, pausing as needed to avoid fizzing.
3. Add food coloring until you get the desired shade of red.
4. Spritz if necessary to keep at the consistency of wet sand, and then place into molds to let dry before storing.

Bath Bomb #45 Lemongrass Twist

Ingredients:

1. 1 Tablespoon Cornstarch
2. 2 Tablespoons Baking Soda
3. ½ Tablespoon Citric Acid, Powdered
4. ¼ Teaspoon Bergamot Essential Oil
5. 1 Tablespoon Epsom Salt

6. ¾ Teaspoon Lemongrass Essential Oil
7. ¼ Teaspoon Orange Essential Oil
8. Yellow Food Coloring

Directions:

1. Mix all dry ingredients together in your mixing bowl first.
2. Add in your liquid ingredients slowly to keep from fizzing. Mix until completely combined.
3. Add in one to three drops of food coloring, depending on your desired shade. Spritz if necessary to keep at a wet sand consistency.
4. Place into molds overnight to allow too dry before storing.

Bath Bomb #46 Vanilla & Apricots

Ingredients:

1. ½ Tablespoon Citric Acid
2. 2 Tablespoons Baking Soda
3. 1 Tablespoon Cornstarch
4. ¾ Teaspoon Apricot Essential Oil
5. ¼ Teaspoon Vanilla Essential Oil
6. Yellow Food Coloring

Directions:

1. Place all of your dry ingredients into your mixing bowl, and make sure it's thoroughly combined.
2. Add one essential oil at a time, and make sure it's mixed completely. Add in these oils slowly to avoid fizzing.
3. Add in yellow food coloring until it's the right color for your preference.
4. Spritz if needed, and then place into molds. Let dry completely before storing.

Bath Bomb #47 French Vanilla Coffee

Ingredients:

1. 1 Cup Citric Acid, Powdered
2. 2 Cups Baking Soda
3. 1 Tablespoon Coffee Grounds
4. 4 Tablespoons Melted Cocoa Butter
5. 1 Teaspoon Vanilla Essential Oil
6. 3 Tablespoons Kaolin Clay
7. 1 Tablespoon Witch Hazel

Directions:

1. Mix all of your dry ingredients together first, making sure it's completely mixed.
2. Mix in your melted cocoa butter next, making sure it's completely combined.
3. Add in your liquid ingredients next. Make sure that you are mixing them slowly to avoid fizzing.
4. Spritz if needed and put into molds to dry.

Bath Bomb #48 Chai Tea Bomb

Ingredients:

1. ½ Cup Cornstarch
2. 1 Cup Baking Soda
3. 2 Tablespoons Epsom Salts
4. ½ Cup Citric Acid, Powdered
5. 5 Teaspoons Chai Tea, Brewed Strong

Directions:

1. Start by brewing your chai tea strong, and then let it cool before using.
2. In your mixing bowl, make sure that you mix all of your dry ingredients thoroughly.
3. Add in your chai tea carefully, mixing completely before placing in molds.

4. Allow for it to dry completely before storing.

Bath Bomb #49 Manly Bath Bomb

Ingredients:

1. 1 Cup Baking Soda
2. ½ Cup Cornstarch
3. ½ Cup Citric Acid, Powdered
4. 2 ¾ Tablespoons Almond Oil
5. 1 Tablespoon Sandalwood Essential Oil
6. 1 Tablespoon Cyprus Essential Oil

Directions:

1. Mix all of your dry ingredients together in your mixing bowl.
2. Mix in your almond oil slowly before continuing once it's mixed.
3. Mix in your essential oils one at a time. Pause to stir to avoid fizzing.
4. Spritz with your solution if necessary to keep it at a wet sand consistency. Place into your molds to dry before storing.

Bath Bomb #50 The Silent Mind

Ingredients:

1. 1 Cup Baking Soda
2. ½ Cup Citric Acid, Powdered
3. ½ Cup Cornstarch
4. 2 ¾ Tablespoons Almond Oil
5. 1 Teaspoon Rosemary Essential Oil
6. 1 Teaspoon Lemon Essential Oil

Directions:

1. Mix in all of your dry ingredients in your mixing bowl.
2. Once mixed, you can then start to add your liquid ingredients slowly. You must go slowly to avoid premature fizzing.
3. Spritz if needed, and then place into your molds.
4. Allow your bath bombs to dry overnight before storing them. They should be completely dry before storing.

Storing Your Bath Bombs

You'll need to store your bath bombs as well. The first thing that you need to remember is that you cannot store your bath bombs until they've been completely dried. Otherwise, you will ruin them. There are just a few things that you'll need to keep in mind when you're trying to store your bath bombs, especially if you're using them for gifts.

Airtight Storage:

Airtight storage is a must. You'll be able to use containers, as seen above, but you also need to make sure that you keep it out of high humidity. High humidity means that there is moisture, and it will activate your bath bombs. So keep them nice, and you may want to give them in such a container even when you're giving them as gifts so that they're in perfect condition when the person uses them.

Keep It Separate:

It's important that you keep your scents separate as well. You may not want to give more than one bath bomb scent at a time, but you still need to keep them separate. You'll find above is a great way to do that. It's not as airtight as you'd like it to be, but it's better than just leaving them open in it. However, the tin container that it's in will help to keep the bath bombs from going bad. Make sure that if you're giving more than one bath bomb, which you'll be marking what they are. Making your own tags is always a good idea. Scents will mix if they are kept together.

Gifting:

Bath bombs make great gifts, especially when you make them yourself. However, you may be unsure how you should package your bath bombs as gifts. Round bath bombs are always welcome, but when you learn to use special molds, it'll help to provide a theme with your bath bombs. This makes them seem even more special.

The use of herbs or petals, as seen above in the heart shaped bath bombs that are great for Valentine's Day, help to make your bath bomb stand out. Some people will also use materials such as glitter or confetti, but this is not recommended for your skin. Stick with natural materials, and you'll still get a wonderful look with your bath bombs. Even when you're making them for gifts.

Keep it in Six Months:

No preservatives are used in these bath bombs, and that's one of the main reasons that they're good for your skin. You'll want to use each bath bomb within six months. Otherwise, the quality of your product will actually go down. Oil and water are in most of these recipes, and so the quality will degrade after this time. You'll get the best quality and the most benefits from bath bombs that are used within this period of time.

Conclusion

You now know how to make bath bombs as gifts and for personal use. Everything from your supplies and how long they can keep has been laid out for you. The only thing left to do is make a quick trip to the store and find what bath bomb recipe works best for you. Just keep in mind you can always tweak the types of oils that you're using in your bath bombs to suit your preference.

You can even balance your oils differently by adding more of one and less of another so long as it is the same amount of liquid as you see in the recipe. Feel free to personalize and experiment to make your bath bomb making experience that much more enjoyable. It's all about having fun and finding out what works best for you.

Printed in Great Britain
by Amazon